Working With Angels

Angels in the Garden

by Nancy Maxwell

Working
With Angels

by Robert R. Leichtman, M.D. & Carl Japikse

ENTHEA PRESS
Atlanta, Georgia & Columbus, Ohio

Introduction

This essay, *Working with Angels,* was first published as part of a set of 30 essays written by Robert R. Leichtman, M.D. and Carl Japikse on *The Life of Spirit.* It can also be found in Volume IV of that series.

It has been selected to be reprinted in this special gift edition because it is probably the clearest, most comprehensive explanation of angels in print. The observations contained in this essay are based on the authors' interactions with angels and angelic forces.

For information about ordering other essays by Dr. Leichtman and Mr. Japikse, please turn to page 96.

Keepers
of the Garden

One of our greatest cultural treasures is the vast number of arboretums, parks, and estate gardens that dot the American landscape, delighting hundreds of thousands of tourists and local lovers of flora and fauna. From spring to fall, these formal gardens are in constant bloom. The shrubs and lawns are kept immaculately manicured and clean. They are a testament to the cooperative achievements of human skill and natural beauty, working in harmony.

To a weekend visitor, such a garden might seem like a magical spot—not just because of its enchanting atmosphere and beauty, but also because flowers and shrubs seem to appear on their own, without the help of human hands or skill. This is not the case, of course. During the hours when the gardens are closed, the staff works hard to prune the shrubs, mow the lawns, transplant mature flowers that have been grown from seed elsewhere, and maintain the physical equipment. Even though we seldom, if ever, see these people, it is easy enough to be aware of their presence. The handiwork they have shared with us is visible testimony to their vision, skills, and labors.

In many ways, life on earth is similar to these gardens. Many aspects of our daily life are obvious and clear to us. These are the events, people, and pressures of daily living. But these aspects of life often have dimensions which are just as much hidden from view as the work force at a botanical garden. Because we do not see or hear them, we are often unaware of their presence. But they are there, interacting with us anyway. Our lack of awareness does not in any way stop them from playing their role in the great drama of the divine plan.

One of the most significant of these unseen work forces is the angelic kingdom—a group of divine workers we have all heard about but probably never seen or consciously known. Angels are like the gardeners of the Eden we call earth; their primary work is to sustain life in the mineral, vegetable, animal, and human kingdoms of earth, even while working subtly to shape these forms and life waves so that they express more and more of the light of the divine vision. But because they work at subtle, invisible levels—even on work days—we remain virtually unaware of them. Even our clerics and theologians, who have claimed angels as their own, know almost nothing about these marvelous beings. So they debate instead their importance in scripture, betraying their total lack of direct awareness.

There is no reason to perpetuate this ignorance any longer. Angels are not only quite real, but are in fact the agency through which life on this planet is sustained. Angels are responsible for building all of the natural forms on earth, from each blade of grass to a whole mountain range— as well as the eyes we use to behold them. Angels absorb the divine forces of vitality and light and then distribute these energies to the forms in their care—be it a pine tree, a tiger cub, a chunk of quartz, or a human being. They work ceaselessly to enact and support the divine plan for the evolution of each life form and each species—as well as for the evolution of whole ecologies, nations, and cultures. Wherever something needs to grow or die, angels will be hard at work—directing, purifying, or withdrawing the life force that sustains the outer bodies.

Angels carry on this work continuously, even though we are generally unable to observe it. This blindness on our part results from the fact that we tend to think of life in terms of its physical forms—its appearance, shape, color, movement, odors, texture, and usefulness. If we cannot see it or touch it, we often assume that it does not exist. Angels, however, do not work directly with forms, as we do; they work with *pure force*—the subtle essences of life and vitality that animate the forms we see.

How important is this continual nurturing of the inner life of all forms on earth? Without this work performed by the angelic kingdom, there would be no life as we know it on the earth. Divine life and intelligence would be unable to manifest in form. The life of spirit would be unable to gather together the bodies it needs in order to appear on earth as a human being. The divine plan for creation could not be implemented.

The crucial role played by angels in planetary manifestation does not, however, lessen the value of the human experience in any way. Through our sciences, arts, commerce, and development of the mind, we are meant to discover how the secrets of earth can be unlocked and used creatively. Ideally, the work of the human kingdom and that of the angelic kingdom are meant to complement each other. Both forms of service have their origin in the intelligence of God, but angels are focused more in the gathering and distribution of the forces of life, whereas mankind is designed more to see how these forces can be translated creatively into works of culture, invention, and civilization.

The forces distributed by angels are similar to that which all of life draws from the sun—directly in the case of plants, indirectly in the case of animals. It is not just one force, but actually many subtle forces, each with a unique purpose. This is because each life form—whether it be an azalea or the Appalachians—has its own design and specific needs. The angelic kingdom is assigned the work of meeting those needs on a daily basis, keeping all forms of life fully charged with the energies and forces they need to survive.

Naturally, the birds and bees and grasses and shrubs of the earth are no more aware, consciously, of the tender ministrations of the angels than the average human is. Nor is there any reason why they should be. But as the average human sloughs off the cocoon of his or her absorption in form, and strives to tread the spiritual path, it does become useful to seek a direct awareness of angels. The work of spiritual aspiration, after all, requires us to become involved in the process of our own healing, growth, redemption, and enlightenment. These basic lessons must be learned first in our own mind and heart—our subtle bodies—before we can use them to help others. These are the very same bodies that the angels work with daily to refine, rejuvenate, and recharge. By learning to cooperate consciously with the angelic kingdom, even to a small degree, we can immensely increase the effectiveness of our personal growth and the spiritual service we provide.

To put this in an even more direct way, we are part of the life of the angels, and they are part of our life. The substance of our minds, our emotions, and our etheric energy system is actually borrowed from the "bodies" of angels. These angelic bodies become our bodies as they are molded and imprinted by our conscious and unconscious values, beliefs, and motives. As the angels continue to pour new vitality and energy through their bodies, we are recharged as well.

The most dramatic illustration of this

interaction between humans and angels at the level of the subtle bodies is the process of birth. Angels are drawn to each new life as soon as it starts to take shape in the womb, providing the substance the new child will require. They hover over the mother at the time of delivery, establishing an atmosphere of serenity and support. For a more thorough description of the work they do in this regard, see Geoffrey Hodson's excellent book, *The Miracle of Birth*.

These same patterns are repeated throughout our life. Angels come to our aid when we need to heal physical or psychological injury or harm. They also assist creative people, not so much by providing ideas, but rather by cloaking our own inspirations with the mental and astral substance that will let us translate our big ideas into successful works of art, music, and literature. Angels also stand ready to assist us at the time of the death of the physical body, permitting our spirit and inner life to be released from the dense human body.

In all of these interactions, the angels act in harmony with the goals and plans of our soul. But since most human beings, even aspirants, are unconscious of the life of spirit, we remain unaware of the co-operation that is occurring.

Even when not interacting with humans, angels work in "response to the plan." They are guided by the force of divine destiny already established for the animal or plant in question. They do not "free lance," as individual humans would probably be tempted to do. They act according to plan.

In some cases, they act in surprising ways. The forces we call the weather are directed by huge angelic forces; massive thunderstorms are a tremendous display of angelic fireworks. Earthquakes are the byproduct of movements by other angelic forces, as they seek to keep the vital forces of Mother Earth in balance. As frightening as these powerful displays can be, however, it is important to realize that they are benign. They are redirecting huge forces in a powerful way.

One of the problems that has arisen in human efforts to understand angels is the notion that humans become angels when they die. This misunderstanding is the result of sloppy theology and sentimental Spiritualism. It is true that when humans die, it becomes more obvious that they are inhabitants of the realms of spirit. But too

many people forget that a) we are inhabitants of the realms of spirit even while
alive physically, and b) the realms of spirit
are filled with many kinds and types of
beings, all of whom would look more or
less the same to the untrained, superstitious
eye. To call a deceased human being an
angel is something akin to calling a cat a
dog, because they both live indoors.

Unfortunately, the term has been used
rather loosely in translating the Bible as
well. In many of the cases where an
"angel" appears and delivers a message,
the messenger was the spirit of a deceased
human being—not a true angel. This does
not diminish the meaning or value of these
messages in any way; it simply clarifies an
otherwise confusing event.

On the other hand, there are a variety
of genuine descriptions of the appearance

of angels in the Bible. When Moses performed his various acts of magic, for
instance, the "pillars of fire" and "fiery
wheels" were undoubtedly angels assisting
in his confrontation with Pharaoh. More
subtle illustrations of angelic forces at work
in the Bible would be the earthquake that
permitted the Apostle Paul to escape from
prison—as well as the bizarre storm that
caused precise, strategic damage at the
time of the Crucifixion.

Actually, angels are described in virtually every major religion. In the Hindu
tradition, for instance, they are known as
"devas" or "shining ones," due to the
effulgence of their light.

The Kabalah, the esoteric teaching of
ancient Judaism, spelled out the names
and duties of the major archangels. In
Colossians I:15-16, the Apostle Paul clari-

fies their relation to the Christ or the World-Teacher: "He (the Christ) is the image of the invisible God, the first-born of all creation; for in him all things were created, in heaven and on earth, visible and invisible, whether thrones, dominions, principalities, or authorities—all things were created through him and for him."

The thrones, dominions, and principalities referred to by Paul are various orders of angels. Some of these vast intelligences are regents of invisible spheres of divine existence. Their lives are so different from ours that it strains the imagination just to speculate on it.

Unfortunately, modern religion has chosen just to pretend that these Beings do not exist, leaving out all references to any levels of life standing between the omnipotence of God and life on the physical plane.

This is a disservice to both human and angelic life.

It is not just the Bible that preserves a record of the angelic kingdoms, however. At the other end of the angelic spectrum from archangels and thrones are the elementals and fairy folk that make up the substance of the angelic realms in the levels of subtle form. Their lives and activities have been chronicled in fairy tales and other forms of folk lore. Although their lives are very much different than that of humans, their interests often do intersect with that of ordinary people—farmers in particular. They have therefore been viewed on occasion by humans who are gifted with some degree of clairvoyance.

Most of these elementals work closely with the elements of nature, especially plant life. They are playful in spirit, yet are shy of human contact. They bring the work of the higher levels of angelic activity down to specific plants, animals, rock formations, and so on. A fuller description of elementals can be found in Dora van Gelder's book, *The Real World of Fairies.*

From shyest sylph all the way to mighty archangels, these beings of light and motion are the keepers of the garden earth. Although invisible to our senses, they work to nurture the forms of life we use and breathe vitality into every facet of our life. All of life on earth is dependent upon the work of the angels for its sustenance.

Angels are God's assurance that the sustenance we need is being provided. Through the kingdom of the shining ones, God continues to breathe life into matter, even as He breathed life into a bit of clay and made Adam.

The Angelic
Link

℘essimists survey the tangible dimensions of life and presume that this is all there is. From this smallminded premise, they then leap to the startling conclusion that creation evolves without significant improvement. Some of these pessimists may grudgingly admit that there have been some achievements and breakthroughs from time to time—but nothing that has improved the quality of life. They conclude that human nature is still the same— meaning just as corrupt and spiritually bankrupt—as it was thousands of years ago. And it will be much the same thousands of years hence.

While pessimism is always chic in circles of specious thinking, it can only be sustained by looking at life—as Paul might have put it—through a keyhole darkly. Pessimists are those who have not yet learned how to climb out of the cave in Plato's famous allegory. For those who have achieved the ability to look at the broader horizons outside of the cave of human ignorance and doubt, there is no ambivalence. They can easily see that God's creation is alive and well, quietly responding to its perfect divine design. In addition, the enlightened members of humanity—as well as the entire angelic kingdom—likewise respond to this perfect design. Through them, God is constantly breathing new life into creation—new vitality, new direction, and new revelations of His plan. Creation is a living, ongoing divine masterpiece.

Most of this vitality passes through the work of the angels. If we behold life in terms that are too narrow, we may fail to grasp the nature and scope of this work. If we think of ourself only in terms of the dense physical body, for example, we will tend to discount any relevance to the need for health and vitality in our minds and emotions. To the dense materialist, after all, thoughts and emotions are just byproducts of the physical life.

This perversion of the way things actually are is a cause of great confusion. Our personality consists of three "bodies"—the dense physical body with its etheric duplicate, the body of our emotions or feelings, and the body of our thoughts, the mind. The personality itself is the vehicle through which the life of spirit refines its skills and expresses its selfhood.

The substance of these three bodies is borrowed for the duration of our life from the angelic kingdom, which nonetheless is able to continue to use it for its own purposes, too. In other words, as we use the mind to think and reflect, our thoughts become cloaked in mental substance supplied to us by the angels. As we build strong feelings of devotion to God or goodwill to our friends and colleagues, our feelings are enriched with the pure substance of angelic love.

In a very real sense, therefore, the angels form a contact with divine life and light, even if we persist in denying it. Our very being and existence is intimately wrapped up in this relationship. Through these ties, and similar ones with the lesser kingdoms of life, the angelic kingdom provides the superstructure for all of life—from the notes of a great symphony to the mineral deposits in a vast desert.   The spark of God ensouls matter, but it is the angelic link that enables spiritual joy to become the bloom of a flower or the smile on a baby's face.

How important is this angelic link? Without it, a diamond would never become more than a pile of carbon dust. We might be moved to express our love for a friend, but have no idea or feeling as to how to do it. This is because we humans, like all other forms of life, must work indirectly with the life of spirit. Although we aspire to the worlds of light, we are often not quite sure what they are like. We therefore depend upon the angelic link to supply us with all kinds of divine energies and ideas that we cannot reach directly on our own.

Angels, on the other hand, are constantly centered in the intelligence and love of God. It is both their design and work to radiate this intelligence and love into those life forms that must operate in the shadows, without full awareness of these inner divine resources. They are the fingers of God as He reaches out to support the sparrow in flight; they are the rhapsody of God as He sings through the heart and mind of a Beethoven or Bach.

Because angels are able to work directly with the divine plan, they are intimately involved in all facets of life on earth. In human life, for instance, they are able to breathe the life force of beauty or joy into the minds and hearts of responsive artists, musicians, poets, and sculptors. Having access to the essence of divine justice, they are likewise able to guide and inspire responsive leaders and lawmakers in our society. They can also be a great source of support for the sick, since they are attuned directly to the patterns of health for all things. Highly evolved angels can in fact embrace the spiritual destiny of a nation and breathe new life into the forces of liberty, justice, and fairness at work in the hearts of its citizens.

Indeed, the scope of the work of angels can easily stagger the human imagination, because it is so vast and powerful. Angels may oversee centuries of evolution for a whole species of animal—or the complex ecological development of life forms within a large geographic region. Some angels work at a planetary level; from our human perspective, their influence is universal. The Archangel Michael, for instance, is the angelic presence of order and justice at the mental level. He affects stability and orderly change in all forms of life, from rocks to humans and even to other angels!

From our perspective, angels are immortal. They may well work on assisting some aspect of the divine plan for dozens of centuries. Their projects may well involve many different species, generations of humans, and immense spiritual and material resources.

It is hard for some people to plan accurately even ten years in advance. Angels often work on projects that will require thousands of years to complete. Our soul can understand this, because it is immortal, too. But the human personality lacks this perspective, and therefore often tries to impose its limitations on its beliefs in angels.

Even limited human beings, however, are helped by angels far beyond their expectation; they simply do not realize it. For those of us who are consciously striving to enter into the life of spirit, the benefit of learning to turn toward the help and companionship of angels can be enormous. Being in tune with divine ideas, the angels are in an unique position to assist us and guide us as we strive to serve the plan of God as best we can.

Some angels specialize in using esoteric sound to aid in the processes of enlightenment and healing. They inspire great composers—such as Mozart, Bach, and Mendelssohn—with magical themes that will awaken humanity to new levels of sensitivity, subtlety, refinement, harmony, and beauty. And even though it may only be the aficionados of classical music that hear some of these compositions, the impact of the angelic ministrations is registered throughout the whole of humanity, helping the entire race develop a greater sensitivity to beauty, refinement, and the life of spirit. Naturally, this impact is something that can only be studied from the inner side of life, not the outer—and it must be measured over a long span of time.

Angels likewise help artists by sharing a portion of their more refined vision or helping a responsive artist sense the inner, subtle dimensions of his or her subject. There can be little doubt, for example, that the great American artist Thomas Cole was inspired by angelic forces to recognize the living vitality of natural life—the angelic presence in nature—and infuse this dynamic perspective into his landscapes. Claude Monet is an example of an artist with a completely different style, yet in his shimmering blends of color and shape, his paintings of flowers capture as much angelic beauty and joy as the massive landscapes of Cole. His paintings convey to us a powerful message—a message penned originally by angels—that beyond the picture itself, there is a subtle but very real measure of beauty and joy within these flowers. As we behold a Monet, the beauty and joy within the painting will speak to the beauty and joy within our own inner life, and help awaken us consciously to a greater awareness of it.

The drawings of Arthur Rackham are another example of artistic angelic inspiration. Rackham became famous for his

illustrations for fairy tales and other chil-
dren's books. With the same impish de-
light often found in fairies, he captured
their essence masterfully in his illustrations. Through his clairvoyant insights, we
in turn are able to get a glimpse of the
realities of life in the angelic kingdom.
Even if we do not happen to believe in
fairies or angels, the message often is able
to sneak by our usual prejudices and
doubts and register at subconscious levels.

The same kind of angelic influence can
be found in great poetry, drama, and
literature—not the kind of writing that
dwells on the ills of life, but rather the kind
that reveals the greater dimensions and
possibilities of life. In writing about land-
scaping, for example, the poet Alexander
Pope urged those who would build a garden to "consult the genius of the place in

all"—in other words, the angelic forces which oversee and support the growth of plants, trees, and animals for this spot. He advises us to cooperate with the intelligence of nature—a clear invitation to work with angelic forces. In his classic mock epic poem, *The Rape of the Lock*, Pope is even more direct; his heroine is consciously assisted by sylphs, undines, and other fairy creatures of the angelic realm. Through the medium of humor, angelic presences communicate to us openly and directly.

As in art, it is not the style of writing that reveals the angelic influence; it is the consciousness of the poet or novelist. There is a huge contrast between Pope's exquisitely refined poetry and the soaring refrains of the chants of Walt Whitman, but they each were blessed with angelic revelation. Whitman is unique in his ability to tap the angelic forces guiding the growth and development of America as a nation. He is more an American prophet than poet.

Poetry is well suited for angelic inspiration, but not its exclusive domain. The novels of Charles Williams ring out with such clarity that it almost seems as though they were written by angels. The same is true of the nonfiction writings of Geoffrey Hodson, especially the series of books he penned describing the angelic kingdom.

Great humanitarian organizations likewise owe much of their original inspiration and sustaining vitality to the work of angels. The ongoing work of the Red Cross is a shining example of the cooperative potential of human beings working with angels. The war relief efforts that followed both world wars also illustrate how effective guidance from angelic realms can be when it is necessary to meet the urgent needs of huge segments of humanity in times of crisis.

Similar patterns of inspiration and revelation can be found in great scientific breakthroughs. This is particularly true in the areas of animal husbandry, horticulture, electricity, and unlocking the potential of minerals. Not only are scientists discovering ways to make our vegetables and animals more fruitful and productive, they are also discovering new ways to use these natural resources to improve the quality of life. The renaissance in the use of subtle energies for medical treatments is a good example of work that is partly inspired angelically. Since one of the basic duties of angels is the direction of force, they are uniquely suited to help us unlock the secrets of manipulating the subtle forces of the body and mind, to accelerate the healing of both.

Naturally, as science becomes more global in scope, the need for intelligent cooperation with angels will become increasingly important.

This kind of global rapport is also important as we strive to serve the destiny of our nation. From the perspective of angels, human society is a divine life wave that needs to be purified, focused, and motivated. Since this kind of work is exactly what angels are designed to do, it is only natural that they are highly involved in shaping the destiny and development of nations. Depending upon the need of the moment, the angelic forces will either be deeply immersed in peacemaking efforts—or they will be busy stirring up rebellion and revolution, when nothing less will cleanse a society of a corrupt bureaucracy and rigid traditions.

For many people, it will be difficult to accept the idea that angels could work through us so readily without our knowledge of it. These are the very people most in need of a new revelation about life, of course—and the least likely to receive it. Like most unimaginative materialists, they assume that what they cannot sense simply does not exist—and what they do not understand cannot work. Yet they have no trouble learning to use television, even though they do not understand how it works—and are unable to see television waves. They somehow manage to accommodate themselves to a widely accepted phenomenon.

In much the same way, we can assume that we do not need the ability to register the presence of angels directly in order to accept them as part of divine life and learn to work cooperatively with them. If we can attune to their intelligence, love, and light, we will be able to interact with them to a surprising extent. And it is to our advantage to learn to do just this, for even the smallest degree of cooperation with angels will enrich our livingness in many wonderful ways. Angels can help us understand more about the life of spirit and how it is designed to function in our life. They can assist us in our creative efforts—as well as our exploration of the inner dimensions of life. And they can be especially helpful in any effort we make to bring renewed health to our loved ones—or ourself.

The challenge of working consciously with angels is enormous. Fortunately, so are the benefits.

Cooperating
With Angels

As Alexander Pope put it, "Fools rush in where angels fear to tread." Whenever we hear of something new, our human nature tends to want to be the first to have it. In our foolishness and arrogance, we sometimes rush into new experiences, new relationships, and even new ideas a bit too rapidly.

This impulsive approach will not work in learning to cooperate with angelic forces, even fairy folk. We cannot demand that they come to us; we cannot lay traps for them and capture them in bottles, like the jinns or genies of ancient fable. They will choose when to approach us, and the conditions under which we will work together.

The key is the very simple word, "cooperation." The angels will not let us boss them around—or experiment with them, as so many scientists are wont to do. They have no interest in satisfying our idle curiosity. They turn a deaf ear to our greed and quest for fame and recognition. But if we have a genuine intent to work in harmony with them, on their own wavelength, then there is no limit to the relationship we can develop.

It is important to understand that the elementary practices of spiritual growth may not work in attracting the help of angels. Simple faith and surrender to spirit may help build a tie between the personality and the higher self, but it is unlikely to attract any angelic forces. Angels do not care if any of us believe in them; they exist whether we believe or not. What they are looking for in terms of human collaboration are spiritual adults who have established spiritual priorities, purified their character, and proven that they can think and act in harmony with the divine plan.

In short, the key to building a cooperative relationship with angels at any level is the ability to engage in creative work of a high caliber—to create in the mode of spirit. This does not mean that we must be an artist or dancer to work with angels. Spiritual creativity embraces the whole range of working with divine ideas and forces to build on earth that which is in heaven.

But even the right intent and right skill

are not enough. We must also create the right atmosphere in which to receive the angelic visitation. If we are preoccupied with worry or anger, no angel is going to want to work with us. If we have damaged our subtle bodies through wanton exposure to hard rock or rap music, no angel will want to be close to us.

On the other hand, the effort to create or perform refined, harmonious music— or radiate loving assistance and support to others—would go a long way toward creating an ideal atmosphere in which to entertain angels of all degrees.

In short, we need to build a strong mental structure of spiritualized consciousness. We must prove ourself ready to work with angels by weaving a tapestry of human qualities that will enable us to work side by side with angels. The contents of this structure will vary somewhat with each person, but the primary qualities that must be included are: wisdom, knowledge, creative talent, enlightened motives, integrity, constant aspiration, steady goodwill, and persistent effort. As we master each of these spiritual qualities, we take another step toward full cooperation with angels. So let's examine each step a bit more fully.

Wisdom is the beginning point. If we are to work with angels and share the forces they wield, we must be capable of responding to the divine design for the work being done. Our efforts must be guided by this inner plan—not by pleasant whimsies or metaphysical speculations. Wisdom is not the product of idle theorizing or public opinion. It is the ability to interact with the divine plan at its own level and retain the clarity of this vision, unclouded by materialistic assumptions, emotional delusions, or ignorant speculations. This ability becomes possible when the individual is able to function at least to some degree as a soul in waking consciousness—that is, when he is able to comprehend the perspective and intent of the soul and harness the personality to express this spiritual intent without distortion.

Even among spiritual aspirants, this measure of wisdom is extremely rare. It is never found among less evolved people. The average human is so stuck in satisfying his or her own needs and emotional comfort that spiritual wisdom becomes impossible. In fact, viewed from the level of spirit, ordinary people are rapidly drowning in the tidal wave of their own sentiments, aware only of what their senses are telling them and missing completely the subtle messages and guidance of the spiritual will.

Wisdom is something more than the accumulated insights of a busy life on earth. It is the accumulation of insight gained as the soul has learned more about the divine plan—its design, purpose, and perspective—and found ways to express these insights through the relationships, challenges, and opportunities to be useful of an enlightened personality. It presupposes a certain amount of mastery in self-awareness, purification of the mind and emotions, and the illumination of our understanding. These, of course, are the achievements of a lifetime dedicated to spiritual living—not just wish fulfillment or theorization.

As wisdom emerges, we gain a spiritual perspective on the vast evolutionary schemes that direct the work of angels. This measure of insight becomes the first link in true cooperation—as well as providing a profound grasp of the awesome scope of the divine plan. It is the kind of wisdom embodied by Thomas Jefferson and a few of the other Founding Fathers of America. They were consciously aware that they were setting new standards for government—a government designed to embody the will of the people while responding to the mandates of the divine plan. Many of the Founding Fathers were strong willed individuals, but enough of them had sufficient contact with the divine intent—and the wisdom to recognize it—to put aside the squabbles and lay a strong foundation for government. As a result, they were able to cooperate both with the divine plan and the angelic forces working upon it to establish a new nation.

Knowledge and creative talent.
To be effective, wisdom must be combined
with knowledge and creative talent—the
ability to connect divine will with our
personal will, divine intelligence with our
human intelligence, and divine love with
our individual love.

The level of knowledge required for
interaction with angelic workers is the
ability to work comfortably and consciously
at archetypal levels, moving back and forth
between abstract and concrete thoughts.
We must be able to define the needs of
humanity and the world in terms of the
divine plan, not just popular opinion.

Our creative talents likewise must sur-
pass the ordinary level, defined as it is by
the expectations of our culture. To work
with angels, we must be able to seize the
solar breeze of an incoming evolutionary

force, comprehend it, and then translate it into a vision we can share with others. It is not uncommon for work of this nature to require several lifetimes to accomplish, especially since the work is not apt to receive popular support, at least in the beginning stages. In fact, we may have to stand against "socially correct" ideas and fads, thereby incurring criticism or even condemnation.

A hint of this kind of creativity can be found in the works of writers such as Charles Dickens or Victor Hugo, whose stories stirred up the latent goodwill in the masses and inspired the intelligentsia of the day to institute long overdue reforms. These writers shook the very pillars of church, government, and the legal sys-tem—not through their own intervention, but by rallying their readers to demand change. In this way, new spiritual light and love was invested into mass consciousness, and through it into the institutions of church, government, and education.

Many people strive to reform society in similar ways, but have not yet developed the knowledge or the creative talent required. They have good intentions and compassion for others, but neither one of these qualities can achieve much all by itself. Only when our compassion and dedication is blended with wisdom, knowledge, and creative skill can we attract the cooperative assistance of angelic forces that we need to succeed.

It is the support of angelic forces that can make one individual a mighty power, indeed.

Enlightened motives are another important element in making ourself ready to cooperate with angels. A motive is any force that impels us to act. In the average person, motives are highly selfish and personal—ambition, vanity, or fear. The spiritual aspirant begins to learn about the need for more refined motives, but mostly just cloaks his personal motives in a spiritual disguise. This is not enough, if we intend to work side by side with angels. Angels are motivated by the divine plan itself. If we hope to work with them, we must make the leap and learn to be motivated in this way as well. We must learn to work and act impersonally.

Some sentimental people misinterpret "impersonal" to mean cold and uncaring. This, however, is a gross distortion of an important spiritual posture. A person who is motivated impersonally is one who is able to work solely for the intrinsic merit of the project, not because he or she is expecting personal glory, wealth, or power—or is trying to atone for a massive amount of fear, guilt, shame, or self-pity. He is motivated only by the desire to be helpful.

The benefit of enlightened motivation is that it frees us to deal exclusively with the work to be done. We do not have to take time off to placate our neurotic tendencies or play a hundred different roles to suit all our friends and enemies. We have the strength to do the work that needs to be done and not be distracted by unimportant side issues.

It is easy to be distracted by unimportant motives—and almost always fatal to our effectiveness as an agent of light or a co-worker with angels. The classic case is that of someone who goes to a lawyer for help in settling a dispute with another person. The lawyer almost always imposes new motivations on the situation—i.e., winning the case, humbling the other side, and forcing them to make concessions. Instead of serving justice, we are now trying to ram it down their throats. The once-neutral motive of trying to settle a dispute becomes clouded with self-serving motives.

This type of distortion is deadly to enlightened work. Angels do not have the kind of personalities capable of vanity, selfishness, or worry. They have no hidden agenda except to serve as a willing and competent servant of divine intelligence. Their fulfillment lies in completing their work, nothing else. They are indifferent to personal affection, flattery, and criticism.

An excellent example of a person who was able to operate with enlightened, impersonal motives without sacrificing his vision was Winston Churchill. For fifteen years, he was out of step with the dominant thinking of England—but he refused to bend in his convictions that Hitler must be contained and deposed. Even after he became prime minister, he was under great pressure to compromise and pander to public fears. Most men would have, just as Neville Chamberlain did. But Churchill remained detached from these pressures, convinced there was only one right course for his country, his king, and his God.

To work cooperatively with angels, we need to strike a similar posture. Our work needs to be motivated by altruistic principles, not our desire for personal gain. We need to be able to complete our work even in the face of disappointment, criticism, and opposition.

Integrity is another indispensable quality to cultivate in anticipation of working with angels. As it applies to spiritual work, integrity is the ability to remain true to the divine ideas that inspire us, and not let them be contaminated or dissipated by popular ideas, trends, or delusions. Richard Wagner, for example, was uncompromising in how his operas were to be conducted and staged. Johannes Brahms destroyed large numbers of his compositions rather than publish anything beneath his standard of excellence. Luther Burbank, the great horticulturist, turned down large sums of money and grand promises and refused to sell out to people who wanted to capitalize on his fame and record. These creative giants all demonstrated an ability to honor and remain true to the source of their inspiration.

This kind of integrity is important because angels are not interested in working through unreliable sources. The strength and depth of one's integrity must be well proven before significant chances to work cooperatively will emerge.

Constant aspiration to the highest must likewise be demonstrated as an integral part of our character. Angels are able to participate in the distribution of divine force because they can identify with it in its highest octave. We live in a world where awareness of the highest and purest is not automatic. We must therefore learn to rise above the lower octaves of human expression and constantly be mindful of the best.

We remain mindful of the best mentally by adhering to the commandment to love God with all our mind.

We remain mindful of the best emotionally by adhering to the commandment to love God with all our heart.

In other words, as we think upon who we are, the work we do, the duties we serve, and the colleagues we assist, we strive always to define these things in terms of their noblest elements. We eschew gossip, rumor, self-pity, and defensiveness in favor of identifying with the cosmic ideal we ought to be serving.

Outstanding examples of constant aspiration to the highest can be found in the lives of people such as Albert Schweitzer and Beethoven. Schweitzer was already a famous musician and theologian in Europe when he decided to study medicine so he could serve in Africa. He gave up a comfortable life of fame and honors in order to serve the plan as he perceived it.

Beethoven continued to compose great music even after he became totally deaf. Others would have used their handicap as an excuse for self-pity and retired from public life. But Beethoven chose not to let a physical deficiency interrupt his spiritual service.

Steady goodwill creates a climate of benevolence which makes it possible to link our consciousness with angels and other spiritual workers. Indeed, goodwill is the keynote on which all spiritual work is generated. This force of goodwill, however, should not be confused for the "warm fuzzies," self-contentment, and nice feelings so commonly touted in spiritual circles today. It is the corollary to aspiration: having identified the highest and noblest within any person, project, or cause, we extend our love and dedication to helping it grow and become stronger. Goodwill is therefore the guiding principle that overshadows our efforts—the atmosphere of gentleness and kindness that helps nurture the work we do.

The power of goodwill is that it shields our spiritual endeavors from the pollution of mass consciousness and the dark side of human nature. It also helps sustain our link with the realm of spirit and the archetypal forces of the mind of God. In a very real sense, it is this aura of steady goodwill that opens the door for true contact and cooperation with the angels. It is also an indispensable attribute for anyone who seeks to heal the sick, whether individual people or society as a whole.

One of the most powerful demonstrations of the expression of goodwill is that of Abraham Lincoln, who demonstrated an unusual measure of generosity of spirit and tolerance even in the midst of terrible conflict. He was assailed by his supporters almost as much as by his critics, yet remained a calm, healing force with a vision of what the United States could become.

Persistent effort is the ability to sustain continual effort in working with angels and spirit for long periods of time. No plan, no matter how noble, and no intention, no matter how divine, means anything unless it produces some measure of transformation or growth. In other words, we must be able to initiate productive activities and guide them toward meaningful results. Heaven must be done on earth.

The need for persistent effort will be immediately clear to anyone who has accomplished any important goal. But oddly enough, there are many people on the spiritual path who do not cherish persistent effort. They believe that holding a spiritual idea or vision in their mind is all they need to do to serve the plan of God. It is not just our duty to ask for greater light and love on earth, as though we were sending in a purchase order to Headquarters. It is our duty to get busy and apply our skills in intelligent, persistent ways. It is our duty to convert enlightened thoughts and attitudes into enlightened productivity.

In fact, the physical plane is the one area in which we can make a contribution that the angels cannot. We have the hands to build with; they do not. They can perform their daily functions without our help, just as we can perform ours, if we choose, without them. But the possibilities that can be achieved if we learn to work together, cooperatively, are so great that it behooves each of us to explore this opportunity more completely.

These are the steps we must master to be able to work effectively with angels. They can be summed up in one key idea: we must *rise up* to their standards of work. We must build a structure of consciousness that enables us to share—to some degree—their cosmic perspective and sense of the universal.

Making the effort to do so opens up not only the kingdom of angels but also the higher levels of spirit as well. It helps us begin to understand the vast power within the divine plan—and the role we are summoned to play in it.

The Presence
of Angels

The opportunity to cooperate with angels, of course, is nothing new; they have been a part of the human experience for many millenia. But most of this interaction has occurred—and still does—without our conscious knowledge. It is the ability to cooperate consciously that is slowly changing, creating new possibilities for the spiritual aspirant. It is not changing because God has had pity on us. It is changing only because more and more humans are developing the ability to work and act as spiritual adults. As this development progresses, so will our awareness of angelic life.

Our knowledge of angels is still clouded by many misconceptions. Some people think that angels quit visiting humans two thousand years ago; others believe that if an angel were to appear, it would be with a crack of thunder, a blinding flash of light, and a deep voice chanting, "Fear not!" As might be expected, however, angels seldom indulge in such theatrics. Their presence can be quite real in our lives, yet at the same time unfelt and unseen. They hover over pregnant mothers to supervise the building of the subtle bodies of the fetus. A different order is on hand at the time of death, making the transition easier for the dying person. These services are offered automatically; we do not need to be aware of them to receive them.

In between birth and death, there are many other ordinary kinds of experiences which might well draw unseen angels to help us quietly. A sincere effort to heal another person or an area of disease in society is one of the most common ways we attract the interest—and help—of angels. A deep love for music—as well as the talent to perform it—would readily draw the attention of the angels of harmony. The sincere effort to teach others and help them grow could likewise attract assistance from these beings of light. Even in times when we find ourself caught up in unjust circumstances, and must take a stand as an agent of justice, we may well be helped by these unseen forces—if we are doing it right.

Doing it right is an important key. If we blame society for our woe, we will repel any angels that might help. If we seek justice as a cover for vengeance, we will likewise cut off any possible support from these realms. If we are motivated only to save ourself, and not correct the larger injustice being served, the angels are apt to leave us to ourself.

It is not necessary to pray or chant to attract this help. As we rise up into our higher self and try to love the ideal we seek to serve—the harmony of our music, the growth of the child, the perfect health of our friend, or the principles of divine justice, the keynote is sounded. The proper order of angels will respond, *provided that we have created an atmosphere that welcomes them.*

This is what most self-appointed reformers fail to do. They are dedicated to change—but are not willing to submit to the divine plan. They are interested in justice—but only for themselves or the aggrieved party they have chosen. They want to help humanity—by forcing it into a mold of their own choosing.

These people will continue to perform their "public service," of course, but without the assistance of angels or other divine resources. They may even become quite famous. But their efforts will not bear long lasting fruit. Often, in fact, it fosters more division and discontent than forward progress.

This scenario changes whenever any of these people awakens to the presence of spirit within them. As they learn to respond to the soul and its plans more than the whims and proposals of mass consciousness, then interaction with the realms of angels becomes possible. Of course, their style of pursuing reform changes as well. Instead of trying to enforce change on others, they learn to inspire others to exercise more responsibility. Instead of advocating revolution, they learn to use the power of proper authority for change and transformation. They learn that the authority to initiate change is derived from the archetypal levels of creation—not the frustrations of mankind.

In other words, these people learn to approach the problems of life creatively. Instead of just recycling old traditions and chasing old goals, they are able to offer fresh ideas and new ways to solve old problems. They become a channel through which the vitality of the divine plan can flow into the earth plane.

It is when this change occurs that people begin to attract the interest of angelic forces, even though they will probably not realize it. The angels help them develop their sense of vision, so that they understand more clearly what the divine plan is trying to accomplish. They may also provide a certain measure of vitality or vigor, so that others will be attracted to the dynamism of the project or activity.

Even though much of this assistance may be rendered without our knowledge, it would be a mistake to assume that co-operation with angels is automatic. Even if we make a deliberate effort to operate on their wavelength, they may make an equal effort to ignore us. We must keep in mind that many human customs are incompatible with the ways of angels. While we may get a kick out of negotiating or presenting complex business proposals, angels may well be repulsed by such hurly-burly scheming. To angels, the thought of getting an advantage over others or haggling over differences is utter nonsense. Such attitudes would indicate that we are not yet ready to cooperate with angels.

Undoubtedly the easiest avenue for becoming aware of the presence of angels is through religious ceremony. Ritual invocation, when properly performed, is designed to draw in assistance from the appropriate order of angels, whether we are celebrating a marriage, baptism, communion, or an ordinary worship service.

This only makes sense. Humanity is apt to be at its highest level of aspiration, goodwill, and wisdom during a time of religious celebration. It is therefore easier for angels to approach. Secondly, the congregation is more likely to be united in a common thought of healing, blessing, or rejoicing, thereby allowing the angels to work in harmony with them.

This does not mean that every religious

ceremony is attended by angels. The celebrant—priest, rabbi, or minister—must be competent and the liturgy must be inspired, as well as inspirational. These conditions occur less frequently than they ought to, but nonetheless the potential is always there.

Ideally, the celebrant will have the strength to lift the rest of the congregation to high enough levels of aspiration that they, too, may sense the angelic presence filling the church or synagogue. Even if the celebrant is unaware of connections with the life of spirit permitting this, his or her devotion to the divine and all that it represents may be enough to make the invocation work.

The role of the liturgy in these formal celebrations is to invoke a divine blessing from God and to evoke from us the qualities of consciousness we need to cultivate in order to honor our communion with the angels—the qualities of wisdom, knowledge, enlightened motivation, aspiration, goodwill, and persistent effort. The liturgy should ask us to acknowledge the authority of divine light and love above all else in our life. It should also give us the opportunity to rededicate ourself to expressing these qualities in all that we do.

There is a real art behind the composition of effective liturgy. If the liturgy is meant to summon angels, the very structure of our invocation needs to create a figurative "funnel" that stretches upward toward the spiritual forces we seek to contact, and downward to provide a conduit for divine force to be poured upon us. As the liturgy unfolds, step by step, it is meant to construct an actual thoughtform of this nature out of the aspiration and devotion of the congregation. If the celebrant is thinking about dinner after the service, however, and the congregation is wondering who will win the ball game that afternoon, the liturgy will fall short of its purpose. As a result, the celebration may not become strong enough to invoke the angelic hosts—nor provide a channel through which divine power can be poured.

Obviously, the more the celebrant and the members of a congregation consciously dwell on the prospect of an angelic presence at their worship, the more likely it is that their efforts will be rewarded. It should also be added that the inability to summon angels does not negate other aspects of a worship service; it is not necessary to attract angels in order to honor God and be guided by the life of spirit.

Nonetheless, the inclusion of angels in any worship service is a powerful way to enrich the meaning of the celebration.

In our daily life, in fact, it might be a distraction to try too hard to contact angels. It would be better just to seek out the assistance of the life of spirit in general and not be concerned with which spiritual agency might answer our prayer. In seeking support and insight at work, for example, we might ask:

May the light of God guide
And the love of God support
The work I do today.

At other times, we might want to focus on a specific quality or archetypal force, such as divine justice or healing. Then we might want to proceed by saying:

May the powers that bring healing and
comfort

Be with the sick and discouraged
To bring strength and healing to mind and
body
Insofar as it is possible.

Or, in the case of a need for justice, we might say the words:

Let divine justice and order
Regulate the affairs of men and nations,
Dissolving divisions and creating harmony.
Let goodwill guide all who would seek
peace.

Of course, these simple prayers could be said by two different people with widely different results. If intoned by an insincere person, for the purpose of impressing others with his piety, the effectiveness of the prayer will be nil. When intoned by a person with a skillfully constructed consciousness of the divine, however, the results will be immediate and powerful.

It is not our belief in spirit and in angels that brings the result, after all. It is our level of consciousness and preparation and readiness. Have we made a dedicated effort to purify our emotions, illumine our mind, and enlighten our lifestyle? If we have, there is much we can share with all facets of spirit, especially angels. But if we have not, our beliefs will remain unfulfilled—until we rectify the omission.

The Vision

On the centuries to come, as more and more people are able to think and act as souls, rather than personalities, there will be greater measures of cooperation between humans and angels. It is part of the evolutionary plan for humans to assist or take over the work of angels in a variety of ways. Healing, for instance, will one day be performed by carefully trained priests who will summon and direct angelic forces to repair human bodies, instead of using medicines or surgery. The regulation of the weather—and much of the problem of pollution—will become possible as enough enlightened people emerge that they can be taught how to summon the various angels who control the weather and the quality of air, water, and soil. Eventually, it will even be possible for fire departments to put out fires by performing ceremonies that compel the fire angels to retreat!

These developments, of course, belong to the far distant future. They are so remote that they serve only to whet our imaginations. Yet they do hint at the tremendous potential that awaits us when we learn to work in harmony with angels.

They teach us something of great importance, too. Where there are fires ablaze in our life—anger that is raging out of control or fear that threatens to consume us—we can call on spirit to put it out. It may not be a fire angel that responds, but the life of spirit is replete with agencies that can douse a wildfire in our own life. Just so, there are other spiritual agencies—and angels—that we can call on to control the inner storms of our moods and emotions. And prevent a few inner earthquakes as well!

Let us therefore learn from the example of the angels. They do not debate theology; they know God. They do not try to coerce one another into thinking as they do; they serve God. They do not try to remake the world; they love God.

We, too, are asked to know God, to serve God, and to love God. And as we do, we will discover something quite wonderful. We share this duty with the angels.

A Complete Listing of the Essays in The Art of Living

Enriching the Personality
The Practice of Detachment
Finding Meaning in Life
Building Right Human Relationships
The Spirit of Generosity
Joy
Living Responsibly
The Nature and Purpose of the Emotions
Cultivating Tolerance and Forgiveness
Seeking Intelligent Guidance
The Bridge of Faith
Discerning Reality
Cooperating with Life
The Mind and Its Uses: Parts I and II
Coping with Stress
Enlightened Self-Discipline
Inspired Humility
The Act of Human Creation: Parts I and II
The Work of Patience
The Pursuit of Integrity
The Way to Health: Parts I and II
The Process of Self-Renewal
Filling Life with Beauty
Becoming Graceful
The Importance of Courage
The Noblest Masterpiece: Parts I and II

A Complete Listing of the Essays in The Life of Spirit

The Spiritual Person
The Spiritual Path
Defeating Evil and Sin
The Power of God: The Mother Aspect
The Power of God: The Son Aspect
The Power of God: The Father Aspect
The Treasures of Spirit
Redeeming Life
Psychic Dimensions of the Life of Spirit
The Role Death Plays in Life
The Trials of Initiation
The Path To Transfiguration
Praying Effectively
Enlightened Confession
The Act of Meditation
Invoking Divine Life
Worshipping God
Making Life Sacred
Finding Heaven on Earth
Linking Earth with Heaven
Harnessing Esoteric Traditions
The Inner Teachings of the Bible
Working with Angels
(seven essays yet to be written)

Ordering Additional Essays

Other essays being issued in Enthea Press gift editions include the two essays in *The Way To Health* ($8.95), "Joy" and "Becoming Graceful" in *Celebrating Life* ($8.95), and *The Role Death Plays in Life* ($7.95). They may be ordered by calling Enthea Press at 1-800-336-7769 or by sending a check plus $2 for shipping to Enthea Press, P.O. Box 1387, Alpharetta, GA 30239-1387.

The rest of the essays are available only in their original form—as one of six essays in each volume of *The Art of Living* and *The Life of Spirit*. These books can be ordered for $8.95 each, plus $2 for shipping. The entire set of either *The Art of Living* or *The Life of Spirit* can be bought for $50 each, postpaid. These books can be ordered from Enthea Press as well.